A STRANGE KIND OF PARADISE

HEARSAY
A
NOVELLA

HETTIE ASHWIN

Published by Slipperygrip 2021

A strange kind of paradise.
Novella: Hearsay
Copyright Hettie Ashwin

All rights reserved

Paperback
ISBN: **9782491490157**
POCKET EDITION
ISBN: 9782956686873

www.hettieashwin.blogspot.com
facebook.com/alacrity.vivacity

Books by Hettie Ashwin

<u>Humour</u>
Literary Licence
The Reluctant Messiah
Mr Tripp buys a lifestyle
Barney's Test
The Truffle War
Fat Bits
Murder! Mayhem! and lesser cuts of meat.
I'd rather glue me nut sack to a bullet train

<u>Memoir</u>
 Boat to Baguette
Living it up in France

<u>Thriller</u>
The Crowing of the Beast

<u>Speculative fiction</u>
The Mask of Deceit
Pi - trilogy bk1

<u>Short Stories</u>
After the Rains & other Stories
A shilling on the Bar

<u>Non fiction</u>
Productive Procrastination

<u>Novella series</u>
A strange kind of paradise 1-4

A mother's trial in life is loving their child.

H.E. Ashwin

All I ever wanted for my son was the best. It's all I ever wanted for Mitchell.

Is that so bad of me?

My husband doesn't understand a mother's love. He can't feel what a woman feels when they have nurtured the life for nine months, given that new person succour and comfort, milk and love. He can never experience that love. Mitchell was part of me. It could never be otherwise.

My son was an independent little boy. He'd wriggle away from his mummy at every opportunity. So much spirit. Headstrong and independent. They are character traits that get you somewhere in life. Roland said I spoilt him, cossetted him. In our rare moments of disagreement my husband threw words around. I knew he didn't mean to hurt. They were only words.

'If loving my child is spoiling him, then I am guilty,' I'd say.

He was a lovely little fellow. Everyone commented on his cherub face, his golden hair.

I enrolled him in kindergarten when he was of eligible age and he and I tried to fit in, but our bond was strong. The other mothers were a bit younger than me. Some had other children in tow, some had jobs to go to. I'd had Mitchell a bit later in life and he was our little miracle. The mothers were polite. They were just not our type. Mitchell and I felt we had a little more finesse, a little more refinement.

It was a three-day week for the little children. I felt it was too much, but the other boys and girls thrived on the singing, the stories, the play time.

I suppose with Mitchell's sensitive nature he was bound to feel different.

He missed his mother, and there was the incident with that little girl. I couldn't believe my boy would push her so violently as to break her arm. It just wasn't like my Mitchell. We graciously withdrew from that small, local kindergarten and thanked our lucky stars Mitchell didn't pick up any other antisocial traits. Roland said I mollycoddled our son. I said he wasn't accustomed to riff-raff. There are always two sides to the story.

I treasured our time together before he would be attending school. It was a special time, never to be repeated.

We'd have mummy time when I would make hot chocolate and we'd read story books, do colouring-in, play silly games. I loved it. He was such a nice little boy. Loving.

'Clingy,' Roland put the word between our mother and son relationship and it stuck there.

I knew school would be rough and tumble. I

knew my boy would grow just that little more and our mummy time would draw to a close. I hung onto my son as any mother would.

Our first day of school was a little less traumatic.

They have prep classes for the children, but I felt Mitchell would have all the prep he needed at home. So, it happened when he was assigned a classroom where most of the children knew each other.

My son looked wonderful in his little school uniform, neatly pressed, shoes shining, satchel on his shoulder. Some of the boys and girls were obviously in hand-me-downs. Not that there is anything wrong with that, and I understand completely the expense involved, but it sets the classroom into the have and have-nots.

The teacher called their names and placed them in desks. I watched from the window as I was the last mother to leave. He sat still and looked every inch the person most likely to succeed. I had high hopes for my Mitchell.

It was about his third week when I was sent a letter.

I didn't expect the letter to be about me.

'Can you believe it?' I showed the letter to my husband. He read it with a growing frown.

'Stay home.' The letter drifted onto the kitchen table.

Mitchell's teacher had the temerity to say I was disruptive to the class. She added that the final bell was 3:27 and not a minute before. If I wanted to wait for my son, I was to do it outside the school gate until the final bell. Peering through the window at 2 pm would not be permitted.

'If taking an interest in my son's education is a crime, put me in prison,' I said to the back door my husband had just exited.

I arranged to meet Mitchell at the side gate. He could see me at a distance and be reassured his mummy was waiting. I'd always be waiting for him.

It was a nasty wet weekend, when Mitchell turned 6. I'd invited all his play friends to his birthday party, but considering the weather I wasn't really surprised it turned to a fizzer. Only the little Italian boy from next door came, with his sister in tow.

I could tell my son was disappointed, but what could I do about the rain I sent the children home with sausage rolls and cake and promised a better party next year.

It was as the little girl was leaving that Mitchell pinched her and made her drop the cake and she started to cry. Mitchell had a devilish look in his eye and Roland, with, what I can only describe as uncharacteristic vigour, lashed out and smacked Mitchell on the back of the legs.

To say I was struck dumb would be an understatement. I felt all of Mitchell's pain, his betrayal of trust in his father – the one person to act as his role model. I felt it as if it had happened to me. The Italian children might get smacked, and often, as I'd heard, but my Mitchell never deserved such treatment. It was a silly boyish prank. The children rushed home. I rushed to Mitchell and Roland pulled me back.

'Leave it June,' he said. I'd only heard that tone of voice once before when I'd tried to explain to Roland's mother the nature of a mother's love. How was I to know Mrs Banner, Dorothy, had miscarried and that Roland and his sister were adopted. No-one told me. No-one let me in on the secret, or the family dynamics.

My husband held my arm and Mitchell went into hysterics. He threw his little body on the floor and denied his mother's comforting hugs, had, what I can only describe as a fit of temper.

'He'll get over it.'

I wasn't quite sure.

Mitchell sulked after that painful episode, but somehow the dynamics in our family changed. It was as if the world tilted just a little in Roland's direction. Mitchell began to gravitate to his father. I felt I was losing my son and to me it was a betrayal. Who was the one to nurture him, feed him, love him like no other. I felt I'd lost Mitchell. I lost my little boy to his father. It hurt.

Roland didn't see it. He wasn't attuned as I was to Mitchell's psyche. How could he fathom the finesse of Mitchell's feeling and emotions? Only a mother can truly know their son.

I put the usurping and Roland's indifference down to Roland being adopted. He just didn't know what it felt like to be blood related to your parents. Of course, he had Mitchell, but he didn't a have a real role model in his own father, Malcolm.

Mitchell wasn't suited to school.

He had a difficult time adjusting to the others. Roland said he should learn the rough and tumble of life, he'd soon get the hang of it.

As his mother I saw it differently. He was sensitive, artistic, possibly a bit of a dreamer. His teachers never appreciated his special talents.

'A talent for skiving and mucking about,' his father said.

I know my son. I knew him better than anyone and I knew he was destined for grand things if only the teachers could see it. They didn't. He was one of those forgotten boys, who they say fall between the gaps.

Throughout his primary years, we were often called to the office. It was always Mitchell Banner's fault. I felt he was their convenient whipping boy. I'm sure he didn't always act independently, but he was the one to shoulder the blame. His teachers threw up their hands.

'We have willing students,' they said.

'We cannot teach one person in a class of thirty.'

'Mitchell needs to concentrate.'

We heard it all.

When Mitchell didn't thrive in school the way we'd imagined, we tried to get him into a Private School. An exclusive education is a big stepping stone to the rest of one's life. People who go to Private Schools are the movers and shakers of this world. They were expensive, but Roland took it all into consideration and we could do it with a small sacrifice here and there. I was willing to sacrifice myself for my son. What mother wouldn't?

It would be the gift of education that would last a lifetime. Mitchell, in such an expensive, rarefied atmosphere could finally shine.

His uniform was a sizable outlay, but he looked every inch the scholar, 'the most likely to', sort of candidate.

The headmaster invited us into his office for an informal chat. He stressed hard work, diligence, and the moral code of the school. I remember looking over to Mitchell and having the feeling that he was really going to get on this time. The Headmaster looked at our son and said,

'It's up to you Mitchell. You are the only one in charge of your future. Use that power wisely.' I thought it was such a stirring speech. If only I had had such a talk at Mitchell's age. My mother always said I was stupid. But if someone believed in me, like this man believed in our son, I could have been anything, done anything. Here was an educational establishment that cherished the individual, nurtured the spirit and mentored young minds.

'Here was $12,000 a year,' Roland said in the car park as we began to drive home. I looked back at the ivy-covered walls, the manicured lawns, the essence that would make a success of my son. I felt I had my faith in the right place.

Mitchell left his old school behind without a backward glance and became a Vaughan Boy.

The money we paid for sporting events, outings, trips to educational events, and the like, convinced us Mitchell was getting a well-rounded education. There was always something going on, some new thing to be paid for, with a permission slip and an envelope.

It was when we were summoned to the Headmaster's office with a phone call on that Wednesday afternoon, when Mitchell was playing hockey at a nearby school, that we were made aware of our son's less than stellar rise at Vaughan.

Mitchell had been missing classes. His grades were less than average.

'Well, it's a wonder,' I said, 'He goes on so many school trips, outings and the like.'

'No, Mrs Banner.' The headmaster consulted his notes. 'His year have only been to the museum once this term.'

Roland looked at me and gritted his teeth.

'What do you mean?' I asked. Roland looked at me like I was stupid. I pulled out my hanky and blew my nose.

'We have sent letters home Mr Banner. You didn't reply. We have repeatedly tried to educate your son Mr and Mrs Banner. Perhaps ...' The Headmaster raised his bushy eyebrows and folded his arms across his chest.

'What are you getting at?' Roland sat on the edge of his seat.

'Our school gives every child the benefit of our many years of experience. We have a reputation for excellence. We have a Prime Minister as an old boy.' He let accolades sink in. 'We also give our pupils one chance to redeem themselves.'

We stared at this man who had our son's future in the palm of his hand.

He had a penetrating gaze that, I imagined, would terrify the students. It felt like he could see right into our hearts and minds. It was a look that laid bare our hopes for our son.

'Expectations come in all sizes,' he said. 'I prefer evidence.'

We left the office under no illusion that Mitchell had been given a lifeline. I wondered if he would take it with both hands.

Our illusions were shattered one evening when we were visited by the Police.

I've never had dealings with the police. I've never had a parking ticket, a speeding fine, not even a summons to Jury service.

A male police officer and a small female officer rang our doorbell at 7:15.

At first, I thought Mitchell had had an accident. It was a natural assumption. Mother's always think these things.

The police stood on our front porch, guns on their hips, badges flashing in the light and asked to

10

come inside.

Roland pushed past me and asked what it was all about. He stood in the doorway and took a puffed-up attitude.

'We would like to know if Mitchell Banner lives at this address?'

'Yes.' I said and added, 'has he been in an accident?' At that the male officer looked askew at his partner and raised his eye brows. I know Roland missed the exchange, but I saw it as clear as day.

'What is it?' I must have sounded a bit frantic, because the female lowered her voice,

'It would be better if we could all just come inside Mrs Banner.' She looked over her shoulder to the neighbours. I understood the nuance immediately. Roland later told me they are trained to manipulate the situation. 'It was a classic move,' he said.

We sat in the front room and I wondered if I should put the kettle on.

Officer Freeman looked too big for our settee. He was one of those Islander types with huge arms and legs. Officer McCall was a bright young woman with cropped hair and crooked teeth. She didn't look much older than our son.

'We have your son down at the Riderstone Station Mr and Mrs Banner. 'I saw Roland run his fingers through his hair. He only did that when he was severely stressed.

'You better start at the beginning.' Roland said, and stood up to pace the room.

It was a hideous tale.

Mitchell has assaulted a boy at school. I didn't believe it.

'It must be a misunderstanding.' I blubbered.

'No. There was a formal complaint, from the parents.' Officer Freeman consulted his notes, 'Mr and Mrs Huxley.'

'Do you know them or their son, Todd?' Officer McCall asked.

'No. We don't know them.' Roland said with resignation in his voice.

'Is …' I swallowed, 'is Mitchell under arrest?'

'No. He is helping us with our enquiries, Mrs Banner.'

'So, when can he come home?' I looked at my husband. He had a sour look on his face. All I could see was Mitchell, frightened, alone in the police station. He needed his mother more than ever.

'We would like you to accompany us to the station Mrs Banner.'

'Me?'

'Yes. Your son is still a minor. We will release him into your care.

'Oh.' I looked to Roland. 'And his father.'

'Either one of you.' Miss McCall said.

We drove behind the police car in silence. Roland was working his jaw into a tight clench and I wrung my handkerchief into a ball.

At the car park I said, 'there must be an explanation. A reasonable answer to all this. I know my son.'

Roland gripped the steering wheel so tight his knuckles went white. I reached over and squeezed his arm.

'Don't touch me.' It was said with a venom I hadn't heard before. I could see he was upset. People do strange things when they are upset. Things out of character. My mother often said she was upset and she'd do things out of character.

I followed my husband into the Police Station and Officer McCall told us to wait.

I was sure it was all some sort of misunderstanding. They would realise he was young, impetuous, prone to bad judgement. It's part of growing up. He must have a good reason to hit someone. We weren't a family prone to hitting. We didn't resort to out of character violence.

We waited for a good hour, watching people come and go, listening to private lives discussed over the counter. Having to talk through a glass screen, made people shout. No privacy, no dignity at all. Roland glowered and took a deep breath. His right leg jiggled. It always jiggled in times of stress.

Eventually we were called into a small room and told to sit.

A middle age man came in wearing a suit and tie. He sat down opposite us, behind the desk and stared. It wasn't a very comfortable feeling, knowing you were being sized up, your parenting skills being evaluated, your love for your son under scrutiny.

'Can we see Mitchell, Mr ...' I left the name hanging.

'Senior officer Duncan, Mrs Banner.'

'Can we see our son Mr Duncan?'

'In good time. You see, your son has been on our

radar for some time Mrs Banner.

'Radar?'

'We know your son is involved in drugs.'

'Drugs.' The word caught in my throat, every mother's nightmare. Roland's leg jiggled manically.

'I don't understand,' I said.

'June,' Roland took my hand and squeezed so tight I let out a yelp.

Mr Duncan sat back and let the pricks of disappointment and shattered illusions get under our skin. It was the death of a thousand cuts. Mr Duncan took his time with us. He explained the surveillance, the workings of the drug culture in our town, the way people get involved and we hung on his sorry tale, looking for any excuse for Mitchell, any small offering that it might not be his fault. The crumbs were few and far between.

Mitchell was sitting in a room, much like the one we had just left. He had a ripped shirt, a bloody lip, just turning purple and looked genuinely worried. I was held back by Roland's hard, firm grip, when all I really wanted to do was wipe away the pain for my boy, sooth the anxiety and make everything right. I was his mother.

'Mum, dad,' Mitchell looked at us and I knew he was sorry for the trouble he'd caused. I could sense his fear at the repercussions.

'What's the story?' Roland stood to attention over our son in the small room.

And Mitchell told all.

Tod Huxley was into drugs. He was trying to sell them to my Mitchell. Well, who wouldn't lash out in such a situation. No wonder the Huxley's didn't want to press the matter further.

We had our day in court for possession of narcotic substances. I didn't even know what a narcotic substance looked like. The senior officer had said young people knew where to get drugs, it was so easy it made his job very hard. He'd seen families torn apart by drugs. He'd seen the worst. I was frightened for my son.

Our humiliation was kept to a minimum as we were scheduled on the same day as the Mayor for fraud. The press wasn't interested in the Banner affair.

He's got another chance,' the Judge said. She leaned over her desk on the dais and looked Mitchell in the eye.

'Take it Mitchell. Take this chance I'm giving you and use it for the rest of your life.' She looked at Roland and I sitting on the benches. 'Mitchell, you have a nice family,' she smiled at us, 'try to do them proud.' I blew my nose in my hanky.

I thought her speech was really rather nice. An older woman who could see promise in my son. She was probably a mother too.

Roland and I had faith in Mitchell. The school saw it in a different light.

The Headmaster didn't send for us to sit down in his office. He didn't ring us and ask to talk. We received a letter on gold letterhead. It said that Mitchell was not the type of student the school wanted to project to the public. Mitchell's grades were not up to standard. Mitchell flouted the moto of the school *'Help others, Help yourself.'* Mitchell's attendance record was less than ideal.

I wondered if we were reading about our son. Roland nodded and threw the letter down in disgust.

I re-read it and down the bottom, in small letters it said there would not be a refund, unless under exceptional circumstances.

'Is this exceptional?' I asked.

'Read on,' Roland pointed.

'*any pupil involved in a police action will not be permitted to continue at Vaughan School for boys.*'

'Oh.'

Roland stormed out of the kitchen and I hoped his shouting couldn't be heard over the fence.

What could I do? Mitchell was a large part of my life and I was bitterly disappointed in his slip from what is good and right. There are times when a mother's love transcends all the heartache, all the worry and anxiety. All I could do was hold my love close to my heart.

I went into the bedroom and pulled out my treasure box. It was my place of refuge in this, sometimes heartless, world.

I looked at a drawing of our family Mitchell had done as a small boy. I was the largest thing in the picture. A blob of a body and large eyes. I was holding a smaller blob by the hand. Roland was a tiny ant like thing in comparison. That picture always gave me comfort, solace.

Another keepsake was the Mother's Day card Mitchell had made for me. It was covered in kisses, love hearts and flowers.

To Mummy, I love you. Mitchell.

That was all he needed to say. My treasure box carried my special bond with my son. I had his teeth, his nail clippings, a lock of hair. The hair was soft as I wiped it on my lips, it smelt of him. And at the bottom was a red love heart. I had made it for my mother for Valentine's Day all those years ago.

I put my treasures back amongst the shoe boxes and Christmas decorations, the bits of material and Mitchell's baby blankets. It was mine, no-one else's.

The back door slammed and Mitchell flew out of the house, Roland's shouted anger clinging to his jacket and disappeared.

I wasn't sure if Roland was angry at Mitchell or disappointed that our faith had been brutally trampled or it all came down to the money. My husband is a no-nonsense type of man. 'It is what it is' is Roland Banner's moto. But he hates to be cheated. Honesty is his guiding principle in life. Honesty is the benchmark in his mind. Roland can put up with almost any amount of trial or tribulation, any amount of inconvenience, but deceit is too much to bear.

'Don't.' He held up his hand at my entreaty when I came back into the kitchen.

He ran his fingers through his hair,

'June,' he began, 'when he comes home, which assuredly he will, don't …'

'What?'

'You know.'

'Love him Roland?' Love my son?'

'You know what I mean.'

I pursed my lips. There was no need to argue.

We'd had this argument more times than I cared to remember, Roland just couldn't see it. He didn't grasp the bond of motherly love. He was a practical man.

And sure enough, my son did come home.
It was around one am I heard the back door open. I slid out of bed and put the kettle on. I could smell drink and cigarettes on him. The smell of alcohol made me gag. I didn't like alcohol. People did stupid things when under the influence. Losing control frightened me. Anything could happen.
'Drinking,' I said trying to hide my disappointment.
'You still up?' Mitchell looked at me through bleary eyes..
'Waiting for you,' I said with measured calm. My son glanced at his shoes then looked me in the eye.
'I'm trying mum. I'm really trying.'
'I know,' I said.
'

Does he hate me?' Mitchell nodded in the direction of our bedroom.
'No.' I said it with conviction.
'Sorry Mum.'
It was all I needed to hear.

Roland and I decided that Mitchell would be suited to something to do with his hands. Something that gave an outlet to his artistic side. My husband put it less poetically saying,
'He's getting a trade if it kills him.'

Mitchell left school without fanfare. I washed and folded his school uniform then put it away in the linen cupboard. It's hard when on-one understands your needs, except your mother.

I suggested a little time to adjust before he began an apprenticeship. Roland said Mitchell was only young once, and that to get a trade they wanted young applicants. 'Pliable youth,' he said.

Mitchell applied to the technical college and we waited. The letter said he was not accepted. They cited his school record. That evening we sat at the kitchen table and contemplated a future for our son. No-one wanted him. I could see Mitchell was incredulous. He always thought he could sail through life, people would accommodate him. Now the real world was beginning to show its cruel side.

'Perhaps we could just get him a job, without the tech college?'

'Don't be stupid June.' I shut my mouth and put the kettle on.

Sometimes miracles happen when you least expect them. We had a phone call from the Tech College. They wanted to see Mitchell, there might be an opening.

A bit of good news is always welcome. We arrived early and sat in the Directors office. He had Mitchell's reports on his desk. I crossed my fingers and Roland jiggled his leg.

A lad had pulled out. There was a vacancy, but ... The Director looked at Mitchell. I held my breath.

'You don't have a good track record Mitchell. There are other people that want this vacancy.

Perhaps they are more deserving.' Roland's leg was in overdrive.

'Do you want it Mitchell?' We all looked at my son.

He nodded and I breathed again.

It wasn't so much a matter of what would you like to do, at the technical college, as there was one place left in plumbing.

'We're not a baby-sitting business,' The Director said. 'We expect results.'

I saw an eagerness in Mitchell. Roland pulled him aside in the car park and said,

'Last chance son.'

We watched our son with anticipation.

Mitchell took to plumbing. I like to think he found his niche. Plumbers make a fortune if they have their own business. They are the new rich and Trades people are a necessity. Mitchell would fit right into that strata of society.

There was a marked difference in our son. I watched as he began to make an effort.

'It's like a light switch has suddenly been turned on,' Roland said. We studied his change and saw the son we had always wanted, emerge.

Here was a boy who could do his best when he put his mind to it. Here was what we had hoped for all along. A boy with his future in his sights.

He would make us proud; we knew our faith was not misplaced.

We had our little differences, but that's all part of growing, maturing.

'Don't mum.' He said it with pleading in his voice.

'What darling?'

'You know. Just don't.' He shrugged off my hand on his shoulder, my pushing his hair behind his ear.

'I just want the best for you Mitchell. Is that so wrong.'

'You're ...' he left the words dangling between us, words that I didn't want to hear and he didn't need to say. I'd watch him from a distance. I knew my son as any mother would. I couldn't imagine my life without him.

Roland would look at me sometimes and narrow his eyes. I'd catch him staring, prying into my motherly instincts trying to figure them out. It unnerved me.

'What?' I said one evening as he studied me.

'June, do you know what you do?'

'What?'

'Do you know? You know, how you won't let go.'

'I don't know what you mean.'

'You do.' He sat forward in his easy chair and tried to prize open my heart with his eyes. Was it jealousy?

'I only want what's best. Is that such a crime?'

'No. We all want what's best,' he said.

'Well, there isn't a problem then, is there?'

Roland didn't answer.

His first year at the tech college felt like a grand achievement. Mitchell had grades that placed him on the eligible list for work.

Roland took us to dinner after that milestone, a special treat.

I looked at our reflection in the glass door of the restaurant and marvelled at the sight. We looked like a normal family, happy, content, and with impeccable manners. All the hard work had paid off. All the ups and downs had made us stronger and the bond of family resilient.

'Happy darling?' I asked my husband when we were getting ready for bed.

He looked at me with a raised eye brow. 'Happy?'

'Yes, are you happy Roland?'

Then my husband said something that bit into my heart so deep I thought I wouldn't be able to breathe ever again.

'Do you love me June?'

I shouldn't have hesitated, but the question took me by surprise. My Roland was a practical man. He wasn't prone to sentimentality, emotional outbursts or touching romance.

Roland turned away and pulled his socks off like I'd seen him do hundreds of times, but this time his back was knotted, scarred from my hesitation.

'Of course I do,' I said, a bit too late.

He put his socks in the laundry hamper and went to clean his teeth without another word. He didn't need to say anything, I could see it in the stoop of his shoulders.

I slipped into bed and reached for my husband. He let me take his hand, a dead gesture.

'Roland,' I whispered.

'Hmmm.'

'I do love you. You are everything to me.' He rolled away from me.

What do you say, what can you say?

After Mitchell's second year with reasonable grades he was offered an apprenticeship. I always knew he would be the one to find a place before the others in his year. It was his natural ability that shone through. He went to work for Henshaw Plumbing, earning a wage, taking responsibility and became a man.

Mitchell looked at us from the back seat of our car. He had a permanent slouch and his hair fell over his right eye. I wanted to tuck it behind his ear, my hands itched, but I laced my fingers together and looked at my husband in the driver's seat.

'Mitchell?' Roland turned and studied our son.

'I'm listening,' Mitchell said while fiddling with the door knob.

Roland impressed upon Mitchell this was his last chance.

'This is it Mitchell. You throw away this opportunity and you will be unemployed and stupid.

I winced. My mother would call me stupid. She said it with a slur and derision in her voice.

'Plain and stupid June.' I knew I wasn't stupid, but I couldn't convince my mother, or even try. I looked at Mitchell, but the word didn't have the weight my memories assigned it.

Make us proud.' Roland took a deep breath and opened the car door.

We stood in reception and waited for 9:30 to tick over on the large wall clock.

'He won't be long,' the receptionist said. We stood around admiring the pipework, the toilet cisterns and the cut away diagrams of pumps.

At the stroke of 9:30 the outer door opened and

Mr Henshaw walked in. His name was embroidered on his overalls and his hat.

'David Henshaw,' he said and held out a meaty hand. He didn't smile and I could tell he wore a permanent scowl like he was trying to figure something out and the answer eluded him.

'This way.' He led us into a messy warehouse full of pipes, tubes, toilets and kitchen sinks. I looked at all the mess and wondered how he ran his business in such chaos.

'In here,' he pointed to a small cubical. We squeezed inside and I took the only available seat near the door. Mitchell put his hands in his pockets and Roland gave him a look that make him take them out again.

Mr Henshaw sat down and pushed some papers over to Mitchell.

'Just sign on the line son.' I winced at the word as Mr Henshaw held out a grubby pen. My son looked at me, then to his father and bent down to put his name on the dotted line. It was just an instant, but I felt as if it was something momentous.

'Right.' Mr Henshaw grabbed the pen and paper and put them in a drawer. He then told us about plumbing.

'We all need drains.' I imagined he used that line more than once. I stole a look at Mitchell. He didn't look like he was listening.

'Now, son. None of that drug nonsense.' Roland and I looked at one another.

'What ya do with ya wages is of no concern of mine, but if its drugs you will be out and at the police station before your blood dries on me knuckles.'

I must have looked shocked, Mr Henshaw frowned at me and carried on.

'I expect you to be on time all the time. If ya sick, I want to see a doctor's certificate. If ya hung over,' he looked at me again, 'That's no excuse.'

I took in the calendar on the wall, a woman who had little or nothing to hide with a wrench.

'That's it then.'

I stood up.

'Hard work, Mr and Mrs Banner.'

We nodded.

Mr Henshaw said he liked to bring lads into the world of plumbing.

'Leave him here and I'll get him sized up for some overalls and tools.' I shot a quick look at my husband.

'He's old enough and ugly enough to find his own way home,' Mr Henshaw said and laughed.

We nodded and left.

'Don't look back,' I said to myself, 'don't look back.'

Roland sat in the car and looked blank.

'Do you think he'll …' I started when my husband took hold of my hand. I looked at that hand holding mine. The wedding ring was worn smooth, the hand had a lifetime of memories. I could see that hand the day Mitchell took it and wrapped his tiny fingers around the thumb. We had made a life and it was hanging onto us for everything. Roland's hand looked so big, so capable with those little fingers gripping tight.

'I'll never let him go,' Roland had said. I remembered the moment so clearly.

Neither will I,' I said.

We sat in the car and held hands.
'Hope. It's all we have left.'
Roland was right. Hope was all we had.

4

Our world was predictable. We watched Mitchell go to work every day, and every day we hoped for the best.

I tried to take a step back. My son had a job, he didn't need a cut lunch. Now and again I'd slip some money into his work pants pocket. Mitchell never acknowledged the gift, or my love. He grew distant, then surly.

'Do you think he's alright?' I asked Roland one evening after my son hadn't eaten his meal and gone straight to his bedroom.

Roland looked over his glasses. I knew that look. Roland often said I was the dumbest person on the planet. It became a sort of joke between us. It was a joke I didn't find particularly funny. He often said I didn't have a funny bone in my body. I couldn't see a joke in a paper bag. I didn't think that was funny at all.

'Well, do you?' I said with a curtness that surprised me. I always thought Roland a bit distant, sometime obtuse, sometimes insensitive. Everyone has their quirks. I waited for a verdict.

'I think Mitchell is just being Mitchell.' His answer didn't satisfy, but it was all I was going to get. We heard Mitchell go out the front door. I hoped he would come back in one piece.

It was a routine that was repeated right throughout his first year at Henshaw Plumbing. I did ask him once,

'Where are you off to tonight Mitchell?' It was said with dread, but I hoped I sounded light hearted.

'Around.'

'Around where?'

'Just around.' He smiled then and I realised my son was quite handsome.

He kissed me on the cheek, borrowed $50 and was gone. I stood in my kitchen and felt my cheek. I wondered if he loved his mother.

David Henshaw and the apprenticeship board sent a report after my son's first year. Mitchell was only doing three days a week on the job and two days study at the technical college. He didn't excel, but neither did he fall behind. The most they could say was he was there when he needed to be. I read that report a hundred times, trying to find something in it that justified the sleepless nights, the worry, the anxious moments, hoping he would find his place in the world, for it was obvious to us that something was missing in our son. The small spark of interest he had shown in his first year had withered and died to be replaced with lassitude and an uncharacteristic indolence. We felt we were losing our son.

'The teenage years are for fast cars, girls and drink,' David Henshaw said when I rang.

'All at the same time?' I must have sounded a bit frantic, because Mr Henshaw guffawed and then said he had to go.

Mitchell was only 16. I watched him assiduously for the signs. All I could see was a propensity for sleep and a reluctance to converse. I had to drag every word from him, like drawing blood.

There was no-one I could consult, no-one I could really talk to about a teenager. Being an older mother, I didn't fit in with the other parents, couldn't connect with their world of three in school and another on the way, juggling a job, a baby, and a home. I tried our local library, but there was nothing that I might relate to Mitchell. The most I could say was there seemed to be a disconnect with us. I wondered if we even existed in his mind. It worried me. It took up a lot of my time, thinking about my son.

My mortification came in Mitchell's second year, just after Easter. A police car pulled up in front of our house, in full view of the neighbours and two officers walked up our garden path. I watched as they rang my door bell.

For a moment I thought I'd hide. I was home alone, at 10am in my slippers with my apron on for the housework; not ready, or in the right frame of mind for the Police. But Mitchell might have been in an accident.

They rang my bell with some insistence.

'Coming.'

What I heard was a story of marijuana. A story of a boy who failed a drug test and was reported to the Police.

The officers acted like they had seen it all before.

I didn't feel that way at all.

'Drugs?' I stupidly said. I could imagine Roland rolling his eyes.

'Yes, Mrs Banner, drugs.' The larger of the officers smirked. I snapped.

'You think it's funny. You think this sort of thing is humorous to a mother? To a mother who loves their son? Do you?' I blew my nose and tried not to cry.

'Mrs Banner,' the smaller officer took a step in my direction and I backed away. 'We would just like to talk to Mitchell. Just talk.'

'Sort of a chat. Young people are impressionable, Mrs Banner. They sometimes need the full weight of the law to see they are on the wrong path.' The hefty fellow frowned and nodded at me.

'Oh, I know all about the full weight of the law,' I said. 'We've been though the full weight of the law; don't you worry about that.'

'Really?' The small one looked at his partner who pulled out a notebook. It was then I saw my mistake. I had alerted them to Mitchell's past.

'If your son could come down to the station this evening … we can have our little chat.'

And they left.

I'm not one to drink, at any time, but I poured myself a small sherry and downed it in one.

My whole day was taken by the looming decisions I had to make. First on the list was the thought of telling my husband. What would Roland say? What would my husband do, or do to Mitchell? I could ring his work, leave a message, tell him Mitchell and I were going out for the evening. It was highly implausible.

And what about my son. If I confronted him,

would he hate me. If I confessed he worried me to distraction would he understand? Perhaps Roland could handle the situation. At least Mitchell could hate his father rather than his mother. I finished the sherry and put the kettle on and had a good cry as I watched it boil.

'Of course he loves his mother.' I said it with conviction. Mitchell knew his parents would be there for him, we were his foundation.

'Roland Banner,' I said to the receptionist and waited on the phone.

'June' I could hear the small nuance of annoyance in his voice.

'Roland, I …'

'What is it, I'm busy. Can't it wait until I get home.'

Yes, I guess it could wait, but I felt Roland should share the worry, the angst.

'No, it can't wait.'

'Well, what is it.' He was curt.

'Mitchell needs to go to the Police station tonight for an interview.''

'What?'

'Mitchell needs to go to the Police station tonight for an interview.' I said and waited.

'What is it this time?'

'I'm not sure. They didn't say.' It was a lie, but once started it felt the right thing to do.

'Is it about his stolen bike?'

'I …' No-one had told me about his stolen bike. My husband was keeping secrets from me. Mitchell was hiding things from his mother.

'Well, no, I don't know.'

'We'll talk when I get home.' He hung up.

Roland had a whole other life from home. He had work people to talk to, friends to go with for a drink after a day at the office. I went to the local library once a fortnight.

5

Roland sat at the kitchen table and looked at his son.

'Any idea Mitchell.'

'No.' Mitchell fiddled with his knife and fork, his hair hiding his face.

'Did they say what time?' Roland looked at me as I tried to busy myself with dinner.

'No. Just this evening.'

I studied my son. He slouched over the table and his fingers kept busy with the cutlery.

'Well, I guess Mitchell and I should go after tea. It's that bloody bike.'

Mitchell looked hopefully at his father.

'When did they steal it? Three weeks, or four.'

'I dunno.' My son shrugged.

Roland stabbed at the mash potato. I wasn't included in the discussion.

'You better get that police number they gave you. The report number.'

I saw Mitchell flinch. Just a small twitch. Roland missed it, but a mother can see the small things. I knew there was more to the story. My mind began to envisage the bike, the money, the drugs. There was no theft. There was no police number.

'Do you think I should go?'

'Why?' Roland looked at me over his dinner.

'Well, I just thought, it's a small matter. I could go with Mitchell. You must be tired.'

'Mitchell and I will go. You don't need to come.'

That was it then. Finished. Done. Mitchell looked at me and I could see the anguish, the pain. He knew his father would hate him after this. I saw it in his eyes.

I watched the car tail-lights until they turned the corner and wished with all my heart life would return to normal. Couldn't we have just a normal family?

It was hours later they returned. I put the television on and picked up a magazine trying to look unconcerned. Roland deposited the car keys in the small bowl near the back door and I heard him go to the fridge.

He came to the loungeroom door and stood there, beaten.

'Where did we go wrong?'

'I don't know,' I said and clicked the television off.

As I lay in bed I wondered what it was that provoked my son. What demon sat on his shoulder whispering in his ear to torment his parents. What reward did that devil tempt my son with to make him do the things he did?

All we ever did was love him.

There must be a shred of decency in my son, somewhere.

Roland rolled over and grabbed for my hand. He hadn't done that in a long time.

'Get some sleep.' He rolled into my neck and kissed me, then took up snoring.

I wondered if Mitchell's demons took a rest. I mused on how fit Mitchell was for the coming battle between good and bad. For one day, he would need to choose. I wondered who would win.

Mitchell lost his apprenticeship.

'We can't have a waister.' Mr Henshaw said to me on the phone. 'There are other lads, other boys that would welcome the opportunity.' I looked at the phone. Roland should be told. It could wait.

Mitchell came home from work and dumped his clothes on the floor, got changed and went out before I had a chance to talk to him. I picked up his things and went through the pockets before putting them in the wash.

It was a letter, scrunched into a ball. It said his appointment was terminated immediately. Three failed drug tests and he was out.

Three?

The woman on the other end of the phone had a nice voice. A calming, quiet voice. The sort of voice a mother might have if she didn't have a son who was a constant worry. I guess the counselling training gives them a voice coach too.

'June, you need to be vigilant. Your son will

exhibit signs. You need to know what they are.'

'How do I know? I don't take drugs. I don't even know what a drug looks like.' I didn't want to sound like I was pleading, but I couldn't help it.

'I can send you a pamphlet if you like. Or you can get one at the police station.'

'Send one here?' I asked.

'Yes.'

'Not here.'

She said I could talk to her anytime. 'Just ask for Tracy.

'Do you have a son Tracy?'

'Yes.' She hesitated, 'and no.' I heard her hand over the mouthpiece.

'June, my son died of an overdose. That's why I do this. I need to help others. Any way I can.'

'I didn't want to cry, but I couldn't help it.'

'You see Tracy. I don't have any friends to talk to. No-one.'

'I understand.' She sounded like she did, really understand.

'June.'

'Yes?'

'How strong are you? Because this is a battle. You need to be stronger than you thought possible.' The silence between us was deafening. 'Sorry, I shouldn't have said that. I'm not supposed to say things like that. They teach you that in the counselling.'

'That's alright Tracy. Can I call you again?'

'Yes.' She gave me her private number. 'June, you are going to war. Are you ready. Are you ready to save your son?'

'I …' I thought about it. 'I'm ready.'

'Harry.'

'Pardon?'

'Harry, my son's name was Harry.'

'Oh.'

'Let's do this for Harry, June.'

'Yes.' I looked at my reflection in the hall mirror. Was I strong? Did I look like I could save my son?

'Tracy.'

'Yes.'

'Thank you.' Now I had an ally, I had a friend.

We went through agonies of lost weekends when Mitchell would disappear on a Friday only to reappear on a Sunday evening throw himself into bed and I could only get a grunt.

I went through the heartache of seeing my son fall apart. He left little bits of that wonderful boy behind every time he came home drunk and all I could do was sweep up the bits from his bedroom floor and press them to my heart.

At his tender age my son was trying too hard to cram a lifetime of experiences into every moment.

'My husband doesn't want to see it.'

'Hmm.' Tracy let me talk as long as I needed. It felt good to get it out, actually say it out loud. It made it more real.

'He's thrown up his hands and called time.'

'Then you must do it June. It's up to you.'

'I know.' I said it with resignation.

'Mitchell will thank you. One day, in the future he will thank you.'

'I know he will.'

Tracy was the only one who knew what I was going through, what a mother's love could do.

It was my challenge. It was my duty.

Mitchell came home at 1am on that Sunday. He was out of it. On something.

I'd been waiting for him to come in the back door. Tracy said getting him when he's just come home was the best. He'd be more receptive.

'Mitchell.' I said it knowing Tracy would back me up.

'What?' He snapped the word.

'This is going to stop now.'

'What?'

'Drugs, Mitchell. The drugs are going to stop now if I must lock you in your room.'

'You?'

'Yes. You will die. Do you know you will die, just like Harry.'

'No.' He slurred the word. 'You don't know shit.'

'I know. I know it all Mitchell.'

My son laughed at me then. Laughed in my face. His contempt for me was like spittle in my eye.

And I slapped him, hard across the face.

I have never laid a hand on my son, but I slapped him, and for one fleeting moment it felt good. He had hurt me so often I'd forgotten how good revenge felt.

Then, before I had time to breathe again Mitchell punched me.

I heard a pop.

6

I don't remember how long he was away before the telephone call.

It was around 6 pm. I'd just served Roland his dinner and the phone rang. It never rings at 6. I looked at my husband and touched the bandage over my eye.

'If it's him, hang up.' Roland played with his mash potato. The phone was insistent.

'Hello, June Banner speaking.' I heard noise in the background, like an office or something.

'Mrs Banner, Police Officer Newton of the West Ridge Police Station here Mrs Banner.'

'Yes.' I looked over to my husband who was pretending not to listen.

'Mrs Banner of …' and he recited my address.

'Yes.' My hands began to shake.

'Do you know a Mitchell Banner of the same address?'

'Yes.'

'Who is it?' Roland barked.

'The police.' Roland threw his cutlery down and yanked the phone from my hand.

'What's this about,' I heard him say.

I studied my husband's face as the officer related

the details.

'Right.' He hung up.

'What is it?'

Roland slumped into the chair by the phone and took a heaving sob. I'd never seen my husband so bereft, so broken.

'What?'

'Mitchell,' he croaked the name.

'Dead?' I said as I slumped to the floor.

'No June, not dead.'

The police met us at the hospital and wanted to know all Mitchell's details. All they had to go by was a telephone number in his back pocket.

I'd always said to my son to carry our number with him, should he get run over. Always carry the number. How many times had I said it to him over the years. The police officer's words, echoed in my mind.

'We found a telephone number in his back pocket.'

'Can we see him?'

'Of course.' Officer Newton smiled. He was a young man with kindly eyes. Someone you felt you could trust.

The doctor was looking at us as we came in, sizing us up as parents.

'He's in an induced coma Mrs Banner.'

I looked at my son. He was bandaged, his eyes black and swollen.

'He's lucky to be here.' Roland took the one

digit we could see and gently stroked our son's little finger.

'It was a great height.' The Doctor fidgeted with the machine that was helping Mitchell to breathe.

'How …' Roland swallowed and tried again, 'will he be alright?'

'Well, that's the question, isn't it? At this stage …' and he went on to explain the injuries sustained from falling from a great height, the impact, the brain tissue, brain swelling and I needed to sit down.

'Cup of tea?'

'Yes, please.'

Roland and I sat in the café and were struck dumb. I looked at the brightly coloured walls, the murals, the pictures of snacks on offer, but couldn't speak.

'Do you …?' Roland stirred his tea.

I knew what he was asking. I couldn't think it of my son.

'I don't know. Perhaps the drugs made him do things.'

'Perhaps,' Roland continued to stir.

'He might have been pushed?' I said.

'He might have.'

We hung onto that thought as our tea grew cold.

As the days ticked over, a routine developed of visiting our son in hospital every evening for an hour, and as we became accustomed to the situation we formulated the scenario that brought Mitchell to this point in his short life.

We said it, thought it, and believed it. Mitchell was pushed, he didn't jump. It was the only explanation that, to us, made sense. The only one we were willing to accept.

Tracy said this sort of thing happened all the time in the underworld. Kids couldn't pay, they were expendable.
'Life is cheap on the street June.'

Sometimes, I wished Mitchell wouldn't wake up, then we'd never know the truth. I couldn't stand feeling guilty all my life. But, I knew. I knew my son better than anyone, and I knew what anguish he must have felt, knowing he had let his parents down.
Yet, somehow his 'accident' had brought Roland and I closer than we'd been in years. My husband was talking to me again.
Perhaps we could be a normal family. Perhaps this was our defining moment for reconciliation.
Tracy said I did what I needed to do. It wasn't my fault he took drugs. It wasn't my fault he hit me. But the guilt was never far from my mind. It sat on my shoulder and whispered in my ear. No-one can fool their heart.

Mitchell came home and I watched for signs of something I knew could rise to the surface. I knew what the depths of depression felt like. I knew what emotional turmoil looked like in a person. I'd been living with it for many years, I knew the signs like I knew the back of my hand.

It was one bright winter morning when I brought Mitchell's breakfast into him that he grabbed my hand.

I looked at the fingers around my wrist. He had my mother's fine fingers, and Roland's long fingernails. How I had studied those hands when he was a baby, touching them, wondering about the life they'd lead.

'Yes.'

'I ...'

'Mitchell.' I didn't want him to talk. I didn't want him to say anything that might upset the fine balance we had over the pit of despair and truth.

'I was a shit, wasn't I?'

'Mitchell, not that word.'

'I was, wasn't I?'

What do you say to your son when he says something like that.

I looked at him.

'You know, don't you Mum?'

He hadn't called me Mum for years.

'I wouldn't blame you if you hated me,' he said.

I touched the plaster cast on his leg.

'I wouldn't blame you at all.'

I decided then to start afresh. A new beginning. We'd be a family again. A normal family. It's all I ever wanted.

7

The doctor said there might be repercussions. Behavioural things that would be out of character.

They sent around a therapist to check Mitchell's cognitive abilities. They scheduled some time with a doctor to 'work through some issues'.

Roland and I watched and waited. We waited for a sign, something to give us hope. Just a little hope for the future. Something to cling onto and hold tight.

It came 6 months after the accident.

Mitchell had popped down to the shops for me. I wanted some carrots for our dinner.

He came inside and I could see a light in his eyes. Something that had been missing was now shining bright.

'You look happy,' I said it with a smile.

'Yeah,' Mitchell grinned.

'Want to tell me about it?'

'Well…'

'Mitchell?'

'Tory. Her name is Tory.'

'Tory?' I said the name and he grinned. My son had fallen in love.

It was as if a light switch had been turned on. Mitchell began to take part in life once more. He began to get up in the morning, make an effort to get dressed.

'Mum.'
'Yes?'
'I got a job.'
'What?' I didn't quite believe it. How could someone get a job, when they hadn't been out of the house for 6 months.
'I got a job. I'm stacking shelves, at night, at the supermarket.'
'Oh.'
'It's good pay. Tory put a word in for me.'
'That's nice.' It felt like I was losing my son once more.
'Next week. I start next week.'
'Are you sure you can do it. It's not too soon is it. Your headaches?'
'Nah. It's all good. I want this. I really want to do this.'
'Well, I'm proud of you Mitchell. That's wonderful news.'

Roland looked at his son across the kitchen table and I saw a pride in his eyes. We had our son back. He was the son we always wanted.
'That's great news Mitchell. Honest work.'
'Yeah.' Mitchell smiled. A light, easy smile that didn't come too often to his face. 'Tory says its easy work.'
'And when are we going to see Tory?'
'Ah. I dunno. Maybe sometime soon.' Mitchell

gave a grin.

'Give the boy a chance June. He's just met the woman.' We laughed then, all of us together, like normal families do. It all felt so right, so very right.

So, Mitchell started his night shift. He would come home and go straight to bed. It was regular, it was routine.

It was about a month later and he didn't come home from work. I waited for him, but I needed to go to the library, so I left the key in our hiding spot.

When I came home my kitchen was a mess, the kitchen table covered in leftover food and the fridge door open.

'Mitchell?' I called. He wasn't home.

I didn't mention it. I didn't want to rock the boat, or make a fuss.

Mitchell resumed his routine, and we all got on with trying to play the part of a happy family.

I'd gone to the shops several times trying to guess who Tory might be amongst the check-out girls. Which one was she? The girl behind the meat counter looked like a nice young woman. The one in bakery was neat and tidy.

'Excuse me,' I said to the woman at the self-serve, 'Do you have a young lady by the name of Tory working here?'

She looked at me and then to another woman at the next checking point.

'Tory,' I said.

'She left.'
'Oh.'

And then I saw her at the park next to the library with Mitchell.

She was wearing all black. She had a ring in her nose, and purple hair.

They looked like they were having fun.

'June don't judge,' I said to myself. She is probably a very nice girl. Purple hair means nothing except she is an individual.

Mitchell looked happy. He was sitting on a swing and gazing into her eyes. He looked like he was in love. My son was growing up.

'So, does Tory have a family?' I tried to sound casual as I served dinner.

'Yeah, they live in Martel Estate.'

'Martel Estate.' I knew about the Estate. It had a reputation concerning the underside of life. Stabbings, murders, all manner of crimes happened at Martel Estate.

'Does she have brothers and sisters?'

'Some.' Mitchell's attention was on eating.

'Some?'

'Yeah.'

Roland shot me a look. The look of old. I knew that look.

A picture began to form in my mind.

Purple hair, fired from her job, Martel Estate and that ring in her nose.

'Does she have a surname Mitchell?

''course.'

'Well?'

'Fuller. It's Fuller.' He finished eating and smiled at Roland.

'Can we meet Tory Fuller sometime?'

'Maybe.'

Roland narrowed his eyes at me and I turned away. Was it wrong to take an interest in my son? We only ever want the best for our children. It's all a mother ever wants.

I began to go through the Estate every day, just to get a feel for the place. If I timed it right I could catch the Fuller family going out. I didn't know if they had jobs. I'd found out where they lived via the electoral rolls. Flat 6 block 6.

The presumed father was first. He didn't take a bag or tools, but left every morning at the same time and walked to the bus stop. Then an older woman, probably Tory's mother. She had a bag and walked into town. I'd yet to find out where she went, because I'd wait until Tory appeared. She was at a loose end, without a job. Dressed in black, with the purple hair she was unmistakable. She'd stride off with purpose. Then there was a young boy of school age. He'd saunter away and I wondered if he ever got to school on time.

One doesn't like to make assumptions, but sometimes a mother can just sense that things will not go well.

I had that feeling. An innate feeling that my son was getting himself mixed up with the wrong sort of people. The Fullers were not for Mitchell. I could see that, and if I told Roland about my feelings, I'm sure he'd see it too.

I watched for a sign that my Mitchell might be cooling on Tory, but he seemed keener every day. He'd splash aftershave all over the bathroom and dash out.

Then, one afternoon when I came back from the shops and they were in the kitchen.

'Mum.' He smiled.

'Oh, hello.' I swallowed and smiled back.

'This is Tory.'

I said all the right things. I said I was pleased to finally meet her and that we'd heard so much about her from Mitchell. He rolled his eyes and smirked. She smirked back. They had a secret code with each other.

Was I on display for their pleasure?

'And what do you do Tory?' I put the kettle on and fussed with my shopping.

'Nothing for now, Mrs Banner.'

She had manners, that was something. But unemployment isn't an idea situation. I could see Mitchell spending his hard-earned money on this girl who was doing, 'nothing for now'.

They left and I heard them laughing on the way out. Obviously I was a source of amusement. And right there I realised what I needed to do.

I would save Mitchell from a terrible mistake. Probably the biggest mistake of his life. What is a mother's love for, if not to protect their children?

8

They were always laughing. It should have given me joy, but it didn't. Tory was polite, and I couldn't fault her on that count, but she'd hang off my son with, what looked to me, like a leech.

Mitchell was smitten. I could see the love I once commanded, for someone else. It was his first love, and I knew enough to know it wouldn't last. First love rarely does. I knew all about first love.

My heart was taken by a boy when I was a young girl. We were in love, we thought the world existed just for us. He was sweet, kind, loving. All the things I craved, he supplied. We made plans for our future, we had the world at our feet, we were invincible together. My mother said I shouldn't aim too high. She said people like me, with a face only a mother could love, with a stoop and no personality should not look for love.

He dropped off the radar. We drifted apart and when Roland came along, he was, my mother said, the best of a bad lot and I should take the chance when I could. It wouldn't come again. I knew all about first love.

I made it a regular event to drive past the Fuller

house. Their lives never varied.

It was raining hard as I pulled up in my usual spot to watch, when a group of youths in black jackets and hoods came whooping up the road and saw me. I have central locking in the car and activated it.

They were splashing in the rain puddles, but their exuberance made me feel uncomfortable.

Whether it was the fear in my face, or my more expensive car for the area I don't know, but they swooped on me. Jeering faces loomed through the windscreen, one boy licking my window. They rocked my car on its wheels and banged on the roof, acting like animals at the zoo. I was frozen. Then as quick as it had escalated, it stopped, and they ran. A face appeared at my window,

'You ok?'

It was Mr Fuller.

'Stupid kids.' He smiled, pulled his raincoat hood a little tighter and walked on.

I could have offered him a lift. I drove home instead.

That close encounter worried me to the point where I was afraid to go out. Did he know who I was? There was no recognition that I could see.

'What's wrong June?' My anxiety was visible, even to Roland.

'Oh, nothing.'

'Is it Mitchell?'

I wanted to tell him about my worry for my son. I could have tried to explain, but a man like Roland wouldn't understand. How could he feel what a mother feels, know how that unbreakable bond works?

'I'm just tired,' I said.

'What's so funny?' It didn't come out in the light-hearted manner I had practiced. It came out like a girl who had felt the mocking behind her back all her life.

It sent Tory and Mitchell scurrying outside in fits of giggles.

'Mitchell,' I called him back, but they had gone.

I watched and waited, and we tried to be a normal family.

Then, one morning, Mitchell came home from work and slammed his bedroom door. That sound was music to my ears.

'Mitchell, darling?' I gently tapped on his door. He didn't answer.

'I could make you a cup of hot chocolate.' He always used to perk up at hot chocolate. When he was convalescing, I'd bring in his favourite biscuits, make a drink. A mother knows.

He grunted.

It could only be because they had broken up, or had a fight.

I knew my son like no other person on the planet. He would be hurt, feeling betrayed, feeling lonely. He would get over it, over her. I was sure of it.

Roland pulled my son from his depression. My husband was terrified that Mitchell would 'do something stupid' again. We never spoke of the event that nearly killed us and him. It was always something stupid, the accident, his time in hospital. Now Roland took my son and tried to build some sort of relationship. They ranged around each other, trying to construct something I knew could never compete with a mother's love. Roland just didn't have the emotional bag of tools that a mother has at her disposal, no matter how much he tried.

And then Mitchell disappeared for three days.

For those three days I watched for a police car. But we couldn't just sit around and wait, even if Roland said he would come home. The accident was our sword of Damocles.

I went to the Fullers.

I sat in my car for a long time watching the front door, before I decided to walk up and knock.

Tory opened the door and looked surprised.

'Mrs Banner?' She said it like I was the last person she expected.

'Can I come in.'

Tory stepped to one side and shot a look over her shoulder.

Their small apartment was clean, neat, tastefully decorated. I had expected overflowing ashtrays, a television permanently on, and dishes in the sink. I didn't think my expectations on what I would find unreasonable considering the estate and its reputation.

54

'Sit down.' She threw another look at a door and sat opposite me. 'Oh, would you like a coffee?'

I said I'd just had one and we looked at one another.

I took a deep breath.

'My son has gone missing.' I let the words sink in and watched her face. She frowned.

'I'm not blaming you Tory,' I said. Although in actual fact I did blame her. She was the cause of Mitchell's anxiety. If he hadn't got mixed up with her, this wouldn't have happened.

'My son is fragile.' And I told her about his accident. I told her about how he has a hard time getting on in life. I explained he was not like other people. He was artistic, a dreamer and these were attributes just as other people had university degrees. She listened with a furrowed brow.

'I know my son Tory. I know him better than anyone.'

'But you don't know where he is.' It was a thrust into my heart with a sword. Those words wounded me as surely as a a a stab.

'Mitchell is my son.' It was the only defence I needed against this girl with purple hair.

'People like you,' I looked around the apartment, 'people like you don't know about the finer feelings in life.'

'Don't we?'

'No.'

We stared at one another. 'I know Mitchell has a magnetism. I can see why you would like him. A mother can sense these things. But he's not for you. He's not like you and can never be like this,' I threw my hands around to take in the apartment. 'He can ...' I could see in her eyes that she had completed the sentence. He can do better.

She studied me and it was uncomfortable. We sat facing one another and then I looked away.

'Mitchell has had some problems, but that's all finished now. He just needed to find his feet.' The silence between us was making me sweat. I could feel a prickle of heat on my back.

'I am here to help my son Tory.' She shifted in her seat.

'I am here to save him from the biggest mistake of his life.' She crossed her legs and folded her arms.

How would Tracy have said it.

'If you see him Tory, it is war, and you will not win.' I let the words sink in.

'Mitchell loves his mother.'

She stood up, a signal that we had finished, but instead of heading for the door she called,

'Mitchell.'

9

My son stood in the doorway and looked at me. I could take just about anything in life, but his look of pity shattered my heart into a million tiny pieces.

'I think you need to go.' Tory opened the front door.

I found myself sitting in my car, it was dark. I had no idea where I was, how I got there or what day it was.

I pulled out my phone and there were no missed calls, it was eight o'clock and Mitchell's face on my screen saver brought me back to that morning. My son stared at me as the time ticked over. I'd taken the photograph when he was in a good mood, after his accident. He looked just like Roland. He had an open, easy face that looked untroubled.

Where had I gone wrong?

I rang Tracy but her phone number was disconnected. She had deserted me just when I needed her. Everyone in my life that I'd cared about eventually left. Roland would too. I could tell our marriage was just a piece of paper. Why we had clung to one another for so long I didn't know.

My solid foundation for a normal family life had crumbled. My son had left me.

I opened the back door to a dark, empty house.
'Roland?' I called, although I knew there would be no answer.

I sat in the dark and waited for the kettle to boil. Was I so bad that my son cast me off? All I had ever done his whole life was love him. Was that so bad?

The kettle clicked off, but what was the point of tea?

I woke up in a hotel room. How I got there I didn't know, but when I looked around it wasn't exactly five-star quality.

There was a television on the wall and tea and coffee making facilities plus a little fridge that was rattling as it worked. There was an empty bottle of spirits on the dirty carpet. I cupped my hand over my mouth and huffed. The smell took me back to my mother, my childhood. I rushed to the toilet and threw up.

I'd slept in my clothes, but what did it matter. Nothing mattered any more. I had lost the one thing I counted on to get me through life.

I made a coffee and watched the television. Life went on and no-one cared. No-one ever cared about June. She was just the one people laughed at, the one that didn't get picked, the one that was dismissed. My mother said I was like wallpaper with a bad pattern. Did Mitchell think I was just wallpaper? Did I really know my son? Did he know his mummy? I had tried, and that's all a mother can ever do.

'Do you love your son?' Tracy had asked. It was a question that didn't need asking. Of course, every mother loves their son.

'Then fight for him.' Tracy had said.

'I did,' I said to the room.

'Fight hard June.'

I parked the car in my usual spot and waited. It was early, too early for the usual jostle of people in the estate. I waited, Tracy's words a banner I could rally to in my war.

I would save my son.

A police car approached and slowed, then stopped. They backed up and cut the engine. I watched as a woman and man got out and walked towards me.

I would say I'm waiting to pick someone up. I'd explain I was an artist, and getting some inspiration. I'd tell them I was an author and looking for colourful identities. Or, I was tired.

The male tapped on my window and make a sign for me to roll it down. I pressed the button and the warm air took me by surprise. Summer was just around the corner. We'd go to the beach. We'd have ice-creams and Mitchell would swim. He'd be happy. We'd be a family.

'Hello Mrs Banner.' He said it with a smile. 'We've been looking for you.'

'Me?'

'Yes.' He peered into the car and waved to his offsider. She came up to the window.

'If you just get out of the car June, we can have a coffee.'

Roland was waiting for me at home. He ushered me into the lounge room and sat me down.

'Thank you,' I saw him say and he blew his nose. I remembered that hanky. I'd bought them so Mitchell could give him something on Father's Day. I always got a token of my son's love, make with glitter and filled with little hearts. Roland got hankies. He saw the police to the door, closed it to turn and look at me.

'June.'

'Shall I make a cup of tea?' Things always took a turn for the better with a cup of tea. It was the one thing to be relied upon in a time of crisis, my mother said. Hers would be laced with 'something to stick to your ribs'.

'We were worried about you?' Roland took my hand and patted it. When had he got so old. His hand had spots on it and the skin was beginning to look like crepe paper.

'Where did you go?'

'Shall I make some scones. I know how much you like scones?'

'June.'

'Yes?'

'You're home now. You can relax.'

How could I tell him I couldn't relax? I had to save my son from making the biggest mistake of his life. He needed me more than ever. I was Mitchell's only hope.

The woman sat on one of the comfy chairs and we smiled at one another. I'd been coming regularly and gradually the pain, the anxiety, the hurt had subsided. What replaced it was a gaping hole.

'How's things?' Angela asked. She extended her hand and I took it. Her dark skin looked like silk. She was young, she had smooth skin. Her battle scars had yet to appear.

'Fine,' I said.

'I hear you're going on holiday soon.'

'Yes.'

'That will be nice for you and Roland.'

'Yes.'

Angela gave a weak smile. I knew what she was thinking. She wanted to pry out my feelings. She wanted to expose my inner thoughts to the light, see what popped up. I wasn't stupid, as much as my mother thought different.

'How do you feel about your holiday?' I said what she wanted to hear and she nodded in all the right places.

This woman who didn't have a clue about my situation, my family, had over the course of visits told me all about myself.

She said I was suffering. But isn't it a mother's lot in life to suffer?

She said I had experienced a breakdown. Who wouldn't when they were trying their best to save their family and no-one was listening to the warning bells.

She said the Fullers were nice people. Mr Fuller was a bus driver, his wife, Margret a cleaner, Tory about to start university as a nurse, their son a model student. They didn't want to ruin Mitchell's life. Pfft, what did Angela know.

I was given pills.

'They will help, June,' the doctor said. Roland asked every day did I take them. He took over the housework, he did the shopping, he tried hard. I wondered why he couldn't see the urgency.

10

I hadn't seen my Mitchell for a long time. Roland said he was deciding to go to university. Mitchell would need to complete some sort of education standard and then it would be set. Roland's words washed over me. They seemed to be doing things behind my back. They were excluding me on purpose, taking me out of their lives, one phone call at a time.

We'd had our holiday, gone through the motions of living, but watching other people having fun was not my idea of a good time. Every happy family was just another arrow to my heart.

And gradually as one day followed another people forgot about June. I slipped into the background noise of life. Angela thought I was ok; the doctor filled my prescriptions by email and Roland stopped looking at me. It was just what I needed to get my son back.

I'd made his room up just the way he wanted and shut the door. He'd want to come home when I explained to him that we could be a family again. He'd welcome me back into his life. I knew it as only a mother could know these things.

It wasn't hard to find the car keys. I took a deep breath. This would be a new beginning.

The freedom to make your own choices is exhilarating. I'd forgotten how it felt just to be behind the wheel and drive. There was no-one to nag me about pills, no-one to slur their hatred at me. I didn't need to hide my mother's bottles of booze, pretend that everything was normal. I was June. I had a son. I was going to save him. It's a mother's role in life.

I parked and waited at the estate. They wouldn't recognise Roland's car, the deceit felt delicious.

I saw him walking with her. She didn't have purple hair now, but a mousey blonde, more natural. And she was wearing bright colours. Mitchell was in jeans and a t-shirt even though it was winter. He always had a strong constitution.

They looked happy, at ease with one another, but I knew different. Tory couldn't know how Mitchell hid his feelings. She wouldn't see the nuance in his eyebrows, the way his mouth turned down at the corners when he was thinking.

He stood and waited while she put the key in the lock and I walked over.

They looked at me with disbelief.

'Hello Mitchell.' I knew he could see my love.

'Hello mum.' He grabbed for Tory's hand and squeezed it tight.

'Mrs Banner.' Tory smiled. 'We thought ... we thought you were on holiday.'

'I'm back.'

'Yes. Er, how was it.'

'Mum, I think you should go.'

He said it with a sadness I'd never heard in his voice before. 'You don't look ... well.'

'I'm well enough,' I said.

They looked at one another and their secret code said more than words.

'Look, mum. Do you want me to drive you home?'

'Yes, Mrs Banner. Mitch will come home with you.'

'That's all I ever wanted,' I said. 'It's all a mother ever wants just to love their child.'

11

People talked over me like I wasn't there. They made decisions for me.

'A slow process,' someone said.

I listened.

Roland came to see me every evening after work. He brought flowers sometimes and little things to cheer me up.

There was always a smile, a wave and a kiss when he left. It's nice to feel wanted, loved.

Mitchell came too. He was hesitant at first, but we had something special. He often brought Troy and they'd sit down for half an hour, looking uncomfortable, then leave.

Sometimes we'd chat about the food, the weather and that sort of thing. Tory would bring me books, crossword puzzles and look at the jigsaws on offer. I thought she'd make a great nurse when her studies were completed. She had a lovely smile. Mitchell was handsome standing next to her. They made a beautiful couple.

I was looked after so well. They really knew

how to look after a person. Angela came. Tracy came. I wasn't a no-body after all. I was somebody.

There was a doctor they told me, that was terrific at helping people work out their past, figure out what was their best assets and fix what needed fixing. He was lovely.

'Hello June.' He breezed in and sat in a chair.

I liked the doctor. He didn't look through me, he could see my worth. I wasn't invisible.

We talked about my mother sometimes.

'I'm not stupid,' I said.

'No June, you're not stupid.' Someone really understood me and it was such a relief.

I recounted some of my childhood and he listened. How I would hide the bottles. How I would pour them down the toilet and replace the vodka with water. How she would lock me in the cupboard, sometimes for days. He listened and understood how it hurt for a mother to say nasty things to a child.

'I loved my child.'

'I know June.'

One afternoon when I wasn't expecting anyone Mitchell came on his own. He sat for a long time, not speaking, then he held my hand.

He didn't need to say anything. We stayed like that, just being close. I knew what it meant. I knew what it took to do that one thing. It took all his love, his strength to reconnect.

I think he'd hated me for so long. I couldn't blame him for that. I just wanted to be the best mother in the world. I'd been waiting all my life to be a mother.

The doctor knew I tried to do my best. He held my hand when I told him about stealing food from the supermarket when I was small, because I was so hungry. He knew I was only doing it to survive. I'd make chips for her and she'd leave them to go cold, and they'd stay on the table for days. I was only six, but I did what I could to keep my mother happy. He knew that.

'Your mother wasn't very good at mothering. She had big problems.' he said.

'I didn't know. For a long time I thought everyone lived like us.'

I went to school sometimes, and other times she wanted me home. She would buy things and we'd play, then she'd get bored and something would set her off. I know she loved me in her own way, but her way often hurt. A burn, a slap and being locked in the cupboard.

In the cupboard I was a perfect mother. I had a small doll that was my perfect child. This was how I would be when I had a little baby. Perfect.

The doctor knew what I meant. He saw it all. He showed me that mothers come in all varieties. We all have different assets when it comes to mothering. I had the most precious asset of all. Love.

'I love my child.' I said.

'I know June.'

There were times when he showed me that

the gift of love included letting our child fly. That mothers can launch their child into the world, leave the nest. I understood that.

He said, 'change tears through everything with the force of a cyclone.'

He said, 'You need just to hang onto the things you want to save, let go of the rest.'

I told him about Mitchell. We only wanted the best for Mitchell. I wanted to be the best mother in the whole world. The one that would always be there for their child. The one that loved him. I said I tried.

'Yes. You did your best.'

'But it wasn't enough?' I said.

'It was more than enough,' he said. And he told me about the destructiveness of striving for perfection.

'We aren't perfect,' he said. 'We're human. We all make errors of judgement. We learn and adapt.'

'Was I bad?'

'No June, you weren't bad. You were a little girl doing the best you could.'

'Am I bad?'

'No. You're human.'

It was one of the nicest things anyone had ever said to me.

And we talked about Roland. How he loved me.

Roland came to pick me up. He looked happy. He held my hand and blew his nose on his hanky.

'Father's day present, remember?' he said.

'Yes.'

My husband watched me as I put my handbag on the kitchen counter. He had his eye on me as I put the kettle on. He studied me as I took the cups from the cupboard.

'It's alright darling.'

'Are you feeling tired June?'

'No.'

'Do you want anything?'

How could I tell him that all I wanted was him, and my son.

'I ...'

'June?'

'I want to live again Roland. I want you.'

Roland had kept the house in tip top condition.

'I've been thinking,' he said. 'How about we move to something smaller? Something more manageable.'

'You mean leave,' I said looking at all the things I had in the kitchen. Mitchell's first cup and saucer. His Winnie the Pooh bowl and plate. His pictures on the side of the fridge.

'Just a thought.'

I found a box the next day and put some of Mitchell's things in it with a label. They would go to the shed. Perhaps one day I'd have grandchildren.

I found my treasure box and wrapped it for Mitchell. He'd probably like more pictures that anymore. I had something I didn't need it the love of my son.

Our new unit was lovely. Smaller, just made for two. We had a spare room and Roland said it might do for visitors, or grandchildren.

'I tried too hard, didn't I?' I asked Roland one evening when we sat at the dinner table.

'You didn't know how June.' He held my hand. I looked at his hand over mine. We were getting older, together. We'd gone through the storm and come out the other side.

'I'm sorry Roland. I just wanted to be better than ...'

'I know.' He squeezed my hand.

'I love you June, always have.'

A strange kind of paradise,
Is the moment of release.
Of battles won
Decisions made
and a conscience at peace.

H.E. Ashwin